HERE COMES CHRISTMAS

A story about Advent

Written by Jenny Gubb

Pictures by Jane Fox

The National Society/Church House Publishing
Church House, Great Smith Street, London SW1P 3NZ

ISBN 0 7151 4800 1

Published 1990 jointly by The National Society and Church House Publishing

© Jenny Gubb 1990

Printed in Great Britain by The Ludo Press Ltd, London SW18 3DG

'Christmas is coming,
The goose is getting fat.
Please put a penny in the old man's hat.'

It was the first Sunday in Advent—only four more Sundays to Christmas—and already Victoria Simmonds was getting excited. Her mother groaned, 'Oh no, don't remind me. I haven't even bought the Christmas cards yet and we've already had one from Auntie Stella. And there's the mincemeat to make and the presents to buy and the cake to be decorated...'

But at least the puddings were made. They squatted heavily on the top shelf of the larder in their white cotton turbans. The cake was maturing richly in the old biscuit tin beside them.

'Can I open the first window of my Advent calendar now, Mum?' 'After you've cleaned your teeth.' Victoria rushed off and scrubbed her teeth especially well. It was very exciting, lifting the little window to find the picture beneath. The picture was of an Advent crown.

They made Advent crowns in Sunday school that morning. Victoria covered a square of cardboard with silver foil and then arranged holly and ivy leaves and pine cones in a circle. She put four lumps of plasticine inside the circle and then fixed four red candles firmly into the lumps.

That night, when it got dark, they put the Advent crown in the window and lit one candle to shine out into the street. It made Victoria feel all tingly inside to see the flame flare and flicker in the darkness.
Only three more Sundays to Christmas.

At school the whole class made mincemeat. They chopped up almonds and cooking apples and weighed out currants and sultanas and suet and raisins and brown sugar, and stirred it all into a lovely mixture with spices and juice from oranges and lemons. Everyone took home a jar labelled 'Class 3 Mincemeat'.

On the second Sunday in Advent, Victoria asked, 'Can I have some of your Christmas cards to send to the people in my class?'
'Why not make some? It would be fun. You could do potato prints.'

So Victoria spent the afternoon carefully carving pictures from potatoes. Her best one was a star of Bethlehem, the star that would lead the wise men to the baby Jesus. She tried to do one of Mary and Joseph and the donkey going to Bethlehem, but the donkey's leg went wrong.

That evening, after supper, they lit two candles on the Advent crown. Victoria's baby brother loved it—he held out his hands towards the flame and gurgled. The candles made a little pinpoint of light in the dark December night.

All next week at school they were busy rehearsing the Nativity play. Victoria's best doll was going to be the baby Jesus and Victoria was going to be a shepherd. She had suggested that her baby brother might be Jesus, but her teacher thought that he might be too wriggly on stage.

On the third Sunday in Advent, Victoria Simmonds' mother was rather irritable. Uncle Basil was coming to lunch and Victoria was taking up the whole table. She was making a Christmas mobile out of last year's Christmas cards. She was cutting out the pictures, smearing them with glue and then sprinkling them with glitter. She was rather pleased with the effect. Her mother was not.
'For goodness' sake! As if I haven't got enough to do.
And look at the baby!'
Somehow the baby had managed to get glue in his hair and round his mouth and over his clothes.
'Kids and cards and Christmas,' screamed Mum. 'And where's your father got to?'

Dad appeared. 'Sorry, I was in the attic, getting the lights. Shall I take them off to buy a tree?'
They went to a place near the station and chose a Christmas tree nearly as tall as Dad. They tied it on the roof rack and then went to the park to give Mum a bit more time.

Mum looked happier when they returned and Uncle Basil had arrived with presents. But they weren't allowed to open them. As night drew in around them, they let Uncle Basil light the three Advent candles. The cosy glow made everyone feel hopeful and close.

The last week at school was very tiring. Mum went to see Victoria in the Nativity play and then there was the school party and the end-of-term concert. And it was Mrs Simmonds' turn to have the stick insects for the holidays.

Then suddenly term was over and it was the fourth Sunday in Advent. At Sunday school they dusted off the thatched stable that had been stored in the vestry since last Christmas. They put the figures of Mary and Joseph and the oxen and the donkey inside, with some hay on the floor. Last of all they put in the empty crib.
Victoria longed for Christmas morning, when the baby would be found lying snuggled up in the little wooden crib.

'Just two more days to Christmas,' said Victoria when they lit all four candles on the Advent crown. The light glowed strongly now that all the candles had been lit.

Christmas Eve was even busier. They had to collect the turkey from the butcher and Granny and Grandpa from the station. Mum made stuffing and bread sauce in between icing the cake, wrapping the presents and feeding the family. She also cleaned the bathroom and made up the spare bed.

Then Mrs Lakhani arrived with a present of homemade sweets. The Simmonds had taken them presents for their Festival of Light in October. It was tea time, so they all had tea together and ate the sweets.

Mrs Lakhani let her son help Victoria and the baby to hang up their stockings. Mum put a mince pie and a glass of sherry on the mantelpiece for Father Christmas.
There was a hush in the house. They were all waiting for that special moment.

The baby soon slept, but Victoria seemed to lie awake for ages listening to the sounds from downstairs and the noises from the street. But she did sleep. Only at midnight she stirred, when all the bells in all the churches across the city pealed out their message of Christmas Day.

Christmas Day! Their stockings were full. There were presents at the bottom of their beds. The baby had a ride in his new car.

Victoria ran to her parents' room. They looked rather dazed.
'What time is it?' asked Mum.
'Half-past five,' replied Dad.
Mum groaned.
The baby began to cry.
Mum groaned again, but Victoria was too excited to mind and she ran off to find the presents she had got for Mum and Dad and the baby.

After breakfast they all went to church. Victoria peeped into the little thatched stable—and there, at last, asleep in the crib, lay the baby Jesus.

It really was Christmas Day.